CW00323073

the Jack Russell Terrier

A guide to selection, care, nutrition, upbringing, training, health, breeding, sports and play

Content

Foreword

The book you are holding is a basic 'owners' manual' for everyone owning a Jack Russell terrier and also for those who are considering buying a Jack Russell terrier. What we have done in this book is to give the basic information to help the (future) owner of a Jack Russell terrier look after his or her pet responsibly. Too many people still buy a pet before really under-standing what they're about to get into.

This book goes into the broad history of the Jack Russell terrier and the Parson Russell terrier, the breed standard of the Parson Russell terrier and some pros and cons of buying a Jack Russell. You will also find essential information on feeding, initial training and an introduction in reproduction. Finally we give attention to (day-to-day) care, health and some breed-specific ailments.

Based on this information, you can buy a Jack Russell terrier, having thought it through carefully, and keep it as a pet in a responsible manner. Our advice, though, is not just to leave it to this small book. A properly brought-up and well-trained dog is more than just a dog. Invest a little extra in a puppy training course or an obedience course. There are also excellent books available that go deeper into certain aspects than is possible here.

About Pets

A Publication of About Pets.

Copyright © 2005
About Pets
co-publisher United Kingdom
Kingdom Books
PO9 5TL, England

ISBN 1852791934
First printing September 2003
Second printing April 2005
Third printing October 2005

Original title: *de Jack Russell Terrier*
© 1999 - 2005 Welzo Media Productions bv,
Warffum, the Netherlands
http://www.aboutpets.info

Photos:
Rob Dekker, Dick Hamer,
Dutch Jack Russell Terrier Club,
The Brittish Jack Russell Terrier
Club The Netherlands, Katja Mink
en Isabelle Francias

Printed in China through Printworks Int.Ltd.

In general

The Jack Russell terrier is an especially popular dog and was for many years a hotly disputed outsider in the dog world. The breed is actually divided into two varieties, the Parson Russell terrier and the Jack Russell.

The Parson Russell terrier has long been recognised by kennel clubs and was judged at international shows according to the British standard. The Jack Russell has only been recognised more recently. Previously it was judged to the Australian standard, but it can now be judged according to the FCI standard. To avoid confusion, the name 'Jack' was taken from the 'Parson Jack Russell terrier'. There are now two recognised breeds, namely the Parson Russell terrier and the Jack Russell terrier. To understand the similarities and differences of the two breeds, we need to go back to their origins.

Origins
Terriers are thought to have descended from small hunting dogs that the Romans brought to Great Britain. They've been used for hunting since time immemorial. They were first used to fight vermin and also learned to go underground (Terra is the Latin word for earth).

Although most people associate terriers with Britain, they were actually first documented in France. Fourteenth century poetry and tales carry mentions of 'terryers' hunting foxes and badgers.

Terriers only became common in Britain in the sixteenth century. While they were first bred as 'general' hunting dogs, breeders later started to breed dogs specialised in certain quarry. Some terriers were masters in tracking down and catching rats and mice, others were specially trained to hunt weasels and otters. By this process of selection for certain traits, various varieties of terriers developed over time. The Jack Russell descended from the fox terrier types and was originally bred to hunt foxes. It was a parson, the Reverend John Russell (1795-1883), who gave this breed its current form. He needed a dog that could work well underground. In 1819 Russell bought a terrier bitch, 'Trump', and she was the first in a long series of dogs that Russell used to create what he felt was the ideal working dog. Only towards the end of his life did the terrier as we know it today come about. 'Jack', of course, is a diminutive of 'John', hence the names Jack Russell and Parson Russell. Over the course of time three different types have developed from that breed:

The Wire-Haired Fox Terrier
This breed was recognised in Britain in 1913.

The working or hunting Parson Russell terrier
Young dogs that seem particularly suited for hunting are selected for further breeding. Generally these dogs stand somewhat taller.

The family pet Jack Russell terrier
Dogs that didn't meet the high standards for hunting dogs were sold as family pets.

In many cases the bloodlines of the three varieties continued to cross, but over time the three breeds differed more and more from each other. Jack Russell terrier clubs were formed, especially in Britain and the United States, but there was absolutely no sign of harmonisation or official recognition. This has only changed in recent times. The Kennel Club of Great Britain recognised the breed on 22nd January 1990 and published an official, provisional, standard under the name Parson Jack Russell terrier (although it actually describes the Parson Russell terrier!). A few months later the breed was accepted by the FCI (the umbrella organisation for Western European kennel clubs). This organisation took over the provisional British standard, but adapted the shoulder

height provisions so that both the taller and the shorter variety were recognised. Only Britain and the Netherlands deviate from the FCI standard and they continued to use the British breed standard with the dimensions for the taller variety. Thus only the Parson Russell was actually officially recognised here until January 2001. In 1987, a provisional register was opened for the Jack Russell, which was then recognised by the F.C.I. in January 2001.

Breed standard

A standard has been developed for all breeds recognised by the Kennel Club for the UK (and in Europe by the F.C.I. - the umbrella organisation for Western European kennel clubs). The Jack Russell terrier is not recognised in the UK, but is recognised by the F.C.I.! The Parson Russell terrier is recognised by the Kennel Club. Officially approved kennel clubs in the member countries provide a translation of the standard. This standard provides a guideline for breeders and inspectors. It is something of an ideal that dogs of the breed must strive to match. With some breeds, dogs are already bred that match the ideal. Other breeds have a long way to go. There is a list of defects for each breed. These can be serious defects that disqualify the dog, and it will be excluded from breeding. Permitted defects are not serious, but do cost points in a show.

The Kennel Club breed standard for the Parson Russell terrier

General Appearance
Workmanlike, active and agile; built for speed and endurance. Overall picture of balance and flexibility. Honourable scars permissible.

Characteristics
Essentially a working terrier with ability and conformation to go to ground and run with hounds.

Temperament
Bold and friendly.

Head and Skull
Flat, moderately broad, gradually narrowing to the eyes. Shallow stop. Length from nose to stop slightly shorter than from stop to occiput. Nose black.

Eyes
Almond-shaped, fairly deep-set, dark, keen expression.

Ears
Small, V-shaped, dropping forward, carried close to head, tip of ear to reach corner of eye, fold not to appear above top of skull. Leather of moderate thickness.

Mouth
Jaws strong, muscular. Teeth with a perfect, regular and complete scissor bite, i.e. upper teeth closely overlapping lower teeth and set square to the jaws.

Neck
Clean, muscular, of good length, gradually widening to shoulders.

Forequarters
Shoulders long and sloping, well laid back, cleanly cut at withers. Legs strong, must be straight with joints turning neither in nor out. Elbows close to body, working free of the sides.

Body
Ribs not over-sprung. Chest of moderate depth, not to come below point of elbow, capable of being spanned behind the shoulders by average size hands. Back strong and straight. Loin slightly arched. Well balanced. Overall length slightly longer than height from withers to ground.

Hindquarters
Strong, muscular with good angulation and bend of stifle. Hocks set low and rear pasterns parallel giving plenty of drive.

Feet
Compact with firm pads, turning neither in nor out.

Tail
Customarily docked.
Docked: Length complimenting the body while providing a good handhold. Strong, straight, moderately high set, carried well up on the move.
Undocked: Of moderate length and as straight as possible, giving a general balance to the dog, thick at the root and tapering towards the end. Moderately high set, carried well up on the move.

Gait/Movement
Free-striding, well co-ordinated; straight action front and behind.

Coat
Naturally harsh, close and dense, whether rough or smooth. Belly and undersides coated. Skin must be thick and loose.

Colour
Entirely white or predominantly white with tan, lemon or black markings, or any combination of these colours, preferably confined to the head and/or root of tail.

Size
Ideal height: at withers: Dogs: 36 cms (14 ins); Bitches: 33 cms (13 ins). 2.5 cms (1 in) above or below is acceptable.

Faults
Any departure from the foregoing points should be considered a fault and the seriousness with which the fault should be regar-
ded should be in exact proportion to its degree.

General Appearance
Male animals should have two apparently normal testicles fully descended into the scrotum.
July 2001

Breed standard printed by courtesy of the Kennel Club of Great Britain

Buying a Jack Russell terrier

Once you've made that properly considered decision to buy a dog, there are several options. Should it be a puppy, an adult dog, or even an older dog? Should it be a bitch or dog, a pedigree dog or a cross?

Of course, the question also comes up as to where to buy your dog - from a private person, a reliable breeder or an animal shelter? For you and the animal, it's vital to get these questions sorted out in advance. You want a dog that will fit your circumstances properly. With a puppy, you get a playful energetic housemate that will easily adapt to a new environment. If you want something quieter, an older dog is a good choice.

Pros and cons of the Jack Russell

The Jack Russell terrier is a 'low maintenance' dog. They don't take up much space, don't eat much and don't need extensive grooming. But 'low maintenance' doesn't mean that this is an easy dog. The Jack Russell is full of temperament, self-willed and imperturbable. After all, these are the traits that make it such an outstanding hunting dog. But its stubborn nature needs a firm hand if you want to keep a Jack Russell as a pet. A correctly brought-up Jack Russell, which knows where the limits are, can certainly be a loyal friend and pleasant company.

Male or female?

Whether you choose a male or a female puppy, or an adult dog or bitch, is an entirely personal decision. A male typically needs more leadership because he tends to be more dominant by nature. He will try to play boss over other dogs and, if he gets the chance, over people too. In the wild, the most dominant dog (or wolf) is always the leader of the pack. In many cases this is a male. A bitch is much more focussed on her master, she sees him as the pack leader.

A puppy test is good for defining the kind of character a young dog will develop. During a test one usually sees that a dog is more dominant than a bitch. You can often quickly recognise the bossy, the adventurous and the cautious characters. So visit the litter a couple of times early on. Try to pick a puppy that suits your own personality. A dominant dog, for instance, needs a strong hand. It will often try to see how far it can go. You must regularly make it clear who's the boss, and that it must obey all the members of the family.

When bitches are sexually mature, they will go into season. On avera-ge, a bitch is in season twice a year for about two or three weeks. This is the fertile period when she can become pregnant. Particularly in the second half of her season, she will want to go looking for a dog to mate with. A male dog will show more masculine traits once he is sexually mature. He will make sure other dogs know what territory is his by urinating as often as possible in as many places as he can. He is also diffi-cult to restrain if there's a bitch in season nearby. As far as normal care is concerned there is little dif-ference between a dog and a bitch.

Puppy or adult?

After you've made the decision for a male or female, the next question comes up. Should it be a puppy or an adult dog? Your hou-sehold circumstances usually play a major role here.

Of course, it's great having a sweet little puppy in the house, but bringing up a young dog requires a lot of time. In the first year of its life it learns more than during the rest of its life. This is the period when the foundations are laid for elementary matters such as house-training, obedience and social behaviour. You must reckon with the fact that your puppy will keep you busy for a couple of hours a day, certainly in the first few months. You won't need so much time with a grown dog. It has already been brought up, but this doesn't mean it doesn't need correcting from time to time.

A puppy will no doubt leave a trail of destruction in its wake for the first few months. With a little bad luck, this will cost you a number of rolls of wallpaper, some good shoes and a few socks. In the worst case you'll be left with some chewed furniture. Some puppies even manage to tear curtains from their rails. With good upbringing this 'vandalism' will quickly disappear, but you won't have to worry about this if you get an older dog.

The greatest advantage of a puppy, of course, is that you can bring it up your own way. And the upbringing a dog gets (or doesn't get) is a major influence on its whole character. Finally, financial aspects may play a role in your choice. A puppy is generally (much) more expensive than an adult dog, not only in purchase price but also in 'maintenance'. A puppy needs to go to the vet's more often for the necessary vaccinations and check-ups.

Overall, bringing up a puppy involves a good deal of energy, time and money, but you have its upbringing in your own hands. An adult dog costs less money and time, but its character is already formed. You should also try to find out about the background of an adult dog. Its previous owner may have formed its character in somewhat less positive ways.

Two dogs?

Having two or more dogs in the house is not just nice for us, but also for the animals themselves. Dogs get a lot of pleasure from company of their own kind. After all, they are pack animals. Although Jack Russell Terriers are very focused on their master and family, they still enjoy more company and being with other dogs.

Jack Russell Terriers can be kept together quite easily. If you're sure that you want two young dogs, it's best not to buy them at the same time. Bringing a dog up and establishing the bond between dog and master takes time, and you need to give a lot of attention to your dog in this phase. Having two puppies in the house means you have to divide your attention between them. Apart from that, there's a danger that they will focus on one another rather than on their master. Make sure that the age difference between the two dogs is approximately two years. This is because the Jack Russel matures quite late mentally (when it is approximately two years).

It is absolutely not a good idea to buy two male Jack Russell Terriers. Two dogs might get along quite well for some time, but if they do start a fight at one point, they will probably never get along again afterwards. Bitches can be kept together quite easily, but you do need to be aware of their character. Never put two dominant bitches together, as you can almost guarantee that this couple will start a fight. Bitches do fight once in a while, but they can normally be left together again after a short time. In practice, there are a lot of breeders who keep several bitches together.

An even better combination is a dog and a bitch, as dogs are quite

happy to endure bitches with an attitude. You do need to bear in mind, of course, that the bitch will come on heat, and that you need to keep the bitch and the dog separated during this time if you want to avoid having puppies.

A dog and children
Dogs and children are a great combination. They can play together and get great pleasure out of each other's company. Moreover children need to learn how to handle living beings; they develop respect and a sense of responsibility by caring for a dog

(or other pets). However sweet a dog is, children must understand that it is an animal and not a toy. A dog isn't comfortable when it's being messed around with. It can become frightened, timid and even aggressive. So make it clear what a dog likes and dislikes. Look for ways the child can play with the dog, perhaps a game of hide and seek where the child hides and the dog has to find it. Even a simple tennis ball can give enormous pleasure. Children must learn to leave a dog in peace when it doesn't want to play any more. The dog must also have its own place where it's not disturbed. Have children help with your dog's care as much as possible. A strong bond will be the result.

The arrival of a baby also means changes in the life of a dog. Before the birth you can help get the dog acquainted with the new situation. Let it sniff at the new things in the house and it will quickly accept them. When the baby has arrived involve the dog as much as possible in day-by-day events, but make sure it gets plenty of attention too. NEVER leave a dog alone with young children. Crawling infants sometimes make unexpected movements, which can easily frighten a dog. And infants are hugely curious, and may try to find out whether the tail is really fastened to the dog, or whether its eyes come out, just like they do with their cuddly toys. But a dog is a dog and it will defend itself when it feels threatened.

Where to buy

There are various ways to acquire a dog. The decision for a puppy or an adult dog will also define for the most part where to buy your dog.

If it's to be a puppy, then you need to find a breeder with a litter. If you chose a popular breed like the Jack Russell, there is choice enough. But you may also face the problem that there are so many puppies on sale that have only been bred for profit's sake. You can see how many puppies are for sale by looking in the regional newspaper every Saturday. Some of these dogs have a pedigree, but

many don't. These breeders often don't watch out for breed-specific illnesses (such as patella luxation) and in-breeding; puppies are separated from their mother as fast as possible and are thus insufficiently socialised. Never buy a puppy that is too young, or whose mother you weren't able to see.

Fortunately there are also enough bona-fide breeders of Jack Russells. Try to visit a number of breeders before you actually buy your puppy. Most breeders are members of the breed associations. These associations also give information on puppies available that have been bred following their guidelines. This will certainly guarantee that you get a healthy puppy, free of any congenital defects. Ask if the breeder is prepared to help you after you've bought your puppy, and to help you find solutions for any problems that may come up.

about the health of the parent dogs or of your puppy. Breeders that are members of a breed association are not allowed to breed with dogs suffering from breed-specific diseases or congenital disorders.

If you're looking for an adult dog, you may want to try an animal shelter. There's a good chance you'll have to search for a while, because shelters don't keep 'stocks' of certain breeds.

Finally, you must realise that a pedigree is nothing more or less than a proof of descent. Most kennel clubs also issue pedigrees to dogs that suffer from a congenital condition, or that have never been checked for them. A pedigree says nothing

Things to watch out for

Buying a puppy is no simple matter. You must pay attention to the following:

• Never buy a puppy on impulse, even if it is love at first sight. A dog is a living being that will need care and attention over a long period. It is not a toy that you can put away when you have finished with it.

• Take a good look at the mother. Is she calm, nervous, aggressive, well cared for or neglected? The behaviour and condition of the mother is not only a sign of the quality of the breeder, but also of the puppy you're about to buy.

• Avoid buying a puppy whose mother has been kept only in a kennel. A young dog needs as many different impressions as possible in its first few months, including living in a family group. It gets used to people and possibly other pets. Kennel dogs miss these experiences and are inadequately socialised.

• Always ask to see the parents' papers (vaccination certificates, pedigrees, official health examination certificates).

• Never buy a puppy younger than eight weeks.

• Put all agreements with the breeder in writing. A model agreement is available from the breed association.

Vaccination plan

If you buy a puppy, a number of vaccinations are advisable:

• at six weeks: puppy vaccination
• at nine weeks: small 'cocktail' (parvo and leptospirosis)
• at twelve weeks: large cocktail (parvo, distemper, liver disease, leptospirosis and possibly rabies).

Even an adult dog (older than one year) must be vaccinated annually:

• in the second year: small cocktail (and possibly rabies)
• in the third year: large cocktail (and possibly rabies)
• in the fourth year: small cocktail (and possibly rabies)
  and so on.

If your dog needs to go into kennels, it must be vaccinated against kennel cough. If you're planning to take your dog abroad, you need to make preparations in good time. Your dog must be vaccinated against rabies and have an identification chip implanted. Consult your vet for details to make sure you can bring your dog back into the UK without it having to go into quarantine.

Travelling with your Jack Russel

There are a few things to think about before travelling with your dog. While one dog may enjoy travelling, another may hate it. You may like holidays in far-away places, but it's questionable whether your dog will enjoy them as much.

That very first trip

The first trip of a puppy's life is also the most nerve-wrecking. This is the trip from the breeder's to its new home. If possible, pick up your puppy in the morning. It then has the whole day to get used to the new situation. Ask the breeder not to feed it that day. The young animal will be overwhelmed by all kinds of new experiences. Firstly, it's away from its mother; it's in a small room (the car) with all its different smells, noises and strange people. So there's a big chance that the puppy will be car-sick this first time, with the annoying consequence that it will remember travelling in the car as an unpleasant experience. So it's important to make this first trip as pleasant as possible. When picking up a puppy, always take someone with you who can sit in the back seat with the puppy on his or her lap and talk to it calmly. If it's too warm for the puppy a place on the floor at the feet of your companion is ideal. The pup will lie there relatively quietly and may even take a nap. Ask the breeder for a cloth or something else from the puppies' bed or basket that carries a familiar scent. The puppy can lie on this in the car, and it will also help if it feels lonely during the first nights at home.

If the trip home is a long one, then stop for a break (once in a while). Let your puppy roam and sniff around (on the lead!), offer it some water and, if necessary, let it do its business. Do take care to lay an old towel in the car. It can happen that the puppy, in its nervousness, may urinate or be sick. It's also good advice to give a puppy positive experiences with car journeys. Make short trips to nice places where you can walk and play with it. It can be a real nuisance if your dog doesn't like travelling in a car. After all, once in a while you will have to take it to certain places, such as the vet's or to visit friends and acquaintances.

Taking your Jack Russell on holiday

When making holiday plans, you also need to think about what you're going to do with your dog during that time. Are you taking it with you, putting it into kennels

or leaving it with friends? In any event there are a number of things you need to do in good time. If you want to take your dog with you, you need to be sure in advance that it will be welcome at your holiday home, and what rules there are. If you're going abroad it will need certain vaccinations and a health certificate, which normally need to be done four weeks before departure. You must also be sure that you've made all the arrangements necessary to bring your dog back home to the UK, without it needing to go into quarantine under the rabies regulations. Your vet can give you the most recent information.

If your trip is to southern Europe, ask for a treatment against ticks (you can read more about this in the chapter on parasites).

Although dog-owners usually enjoy taking their dog on holiday, you must seriously ask yourself whether the dog feels that way too. Jack Russells certainly don't always feel comfortable in a hot country. Days spent travelling in a car are also often not their preference, and some dogs suffer badly from car-sickness. There are good medicines for this, but it's questionable whether you're doing your

dog a favour with them. If you do decide to take it with you, make regular stops at safe places during your journey, so that your dog can have a good run. Take plenty of fresh drinking water with you, as well as the food your dog is used to. Don't leave your dog in a car that is parked in the sun. It can quickly be overcome by the heat, with even fatal consequences. If you can't avoid it, park the car in the shade if at all possible, and leave a window open for a little fresh air. Even if you've taken these precautions, never stay away long!

If you're travelling by plane or ship, make your travel plans in time to ensure that your dog can travel with you and that the necessary rules are observed. You will need some time to make all the arrangements. Should you decide not to take your dog with you, you then need to find somewhere for it to stay. Arrangements for a place in kennels need to be made well in advance, and there may be certain vaccinations required, which need to be given a minimum of one month before the stay.

If your dog can't be accommodated in the homes of relatives or friends, it might be possible to have an acquaintance stay in your house. This also needs to be arranged well in advance, as it may be difficult to find someone who can do this.

Always ensure that your dog can be traced should it run away or get lost while on holiday. A little tube with your address or a tag with home and holiday address can avoid a lot of problems.

Moving home

Dogs generally become more attached to humans than to the house they live in. Moving home is usually not a problem for them. But it can be useful before moving to let the dog get to know its new home and the area around it.

If you can, leave your dog with relatives or friends (or in kennels) on the day of the move. The chance of it running away or getting lost is then practically non-

existent. When your move is complete, you can pick up your dog and let it quietly get familiar with its new home and environment. Give it its own place in the house at once and it will quickly adapt. During the first week or so, always walk your dog on a lead because an animal can also get lost in new surroundings. Always take a different route so it quickly gets to know the neighbourhood.

Don't forget to get your new address and phone number engraved on the dog's tag. Send a change of address notice to the chip or tattoo registration office. Dogs must sometimes be registered in a new community.

Nutrition, feeding your Jack Russel

A dog will actually eat a lot more than just meat. In the wild it would eat its prey complete with skin and fur, including the bones, stomach, and the innards with their semi-digested vegetable material.

In this way the dog supplements its meat menu with the vitamins and minerals it needs. This is also the basis for feeding a domestic dog.

Ready-made foods

It's not easy for a layman to put together a complete menu for a dog, which includes all the necessary proteins, fats, vitamins and minerals in just the right proportions and quantities. Meat alone is certainly not a complete meal for a dog. It contains too little calcium. A calcium deficiency over time will lead to bone defects, and for a fast-growing puppy this can lead to serious skeletal deformities.

If you mix its food yourself, you can easily give your dog too much in terms of vitamins and minerals, which can also be bad for your dog's health. You can avoid these problems by giving it ready-made food of a good brand. These products are well-balanced and contain everything your dog needs. Supplements such as vitamin preparations are superfluous. The amount of food your dog needs depends on its weight and activity level. You can find guidelines on the packaging. Split the food into two meals per day if possible, and always ensure there's a dish of fresh drinking water next to its food.

Give your dog the time to digest its food, don't let it outside straight after a meal. A dog should also never play on a full stomach. This can cause stomach torsion (the stomach turning over), which can be fatal for your dog. Because the nutritional needs of a dog depend, among other things, on its age and way of life, there are many different types of dog food available. There are "light" foods for less active dogs, "energy" foods for working dogs and "senior" foods for the older dog.

Canned foods, mixer and dry foods

Ready-made foods available at pet shops or in the supermarket can roughly be split into canned food, mixer and dry food. Whichever form you choose, ensure that it's a complete food with all the necessary ingredients. You can see this on the packaging.

Most dogs love canned food. Although the better brands are composed well, they do have one disadvantage: they are soft. A dog fed only on canned food will sooner or later have problems with its teeth (plaque, paradontosis). Besides canned food, give your dog hard foods at certain times or a dog chew such as Nylabone Healthy Edibles. Mixer is a food consisting of chunks, dried vegetables and grains. Almost all moisture has been extracted. The advantages of mixer are that it is light and keeps well. You add a certain amount of water and the meal is ready. A disadvantage is that it must definitely not be fed without

water. Without the extra fluid, mixer will absorb the fluids present in the stomach, with serious results. Should your dog manage to get at the bag and enjoy its contents, you must immediately give it plenty to drink. Dry chunks have also had the moisture extracted but not as much as mixer. The advantage of dry foods is that they are hard, forcing the dog to use its jaws, removing plaque and massaging the gums.

Dog chew products

Of course, once in a while you want to spoil your dog with something extra. Don't give it pieces of cheese or sausage as these contain too much salt and fat. There are various products available that a dog will find delicious and which are also healthy, especially for its teeth. You'll find a large range of varying quality in the pet shop.

The butcher's left-overs

The bones of slaughtered animals have traditionally been given to the dog, and dogs love them, but they are not without risks. Pork and poultry bones are too weak. They can splinter and cause serious injury to the intestines. Beef bones are more suitable, but they must first be cooked to kill off dangerous bacteria. Pet shops carry a range of smoked, cooked and dried abattoir residue, such as pigs' ears, bull penis, tripe sticks,

oxtails, gullet, dried muscle meat, and hoof chews.

Fresh meat
If you do want to give your dog fresh meat occasionally, never give it raw, but always boiled or roasted. Raw (or not fully cooked) pork or chicken can contain life-threatening bacteria. Chicken can be contaminated by the notorious salmonella bacteria, while pork can carry the Aujeszky virus. This disease is incurable and will quickly lead to the death of your pet.

Buffalo hide or cowhide chews
Dog chews are mostly made of beef or buffalo hide. Chews are usually knotted or pressed hide and can come in the form of little shoes, twisted sticks, lollies, balls and various other shapes; nice to look at and a nice change.

Munchy sticks

Munchy sticks are green, yellow, red or brown coloured sticks of various thicknesses. They consist of ground buffalo hide with a number of often undefined additives. The composition and quality of these between-meal treats is not always clear. Some are fine, but there have also been sticks found to contain high levels of cardboard and even paint residues. Choose a product whose ingredients are clearly described.

Overweight?

Recent investigations have shown that many dogs are overweight. A dog usually gets too fat because of over-feeding and lack of exercise. Use of medicines or a disease is rarely the cause. Dogs that get too fat are often given too much food or too many treats between meals. Gluttony or boredom can also be a cause, and a dog often puts on weight following castration or sterilisation. Due to changes in hormone levels it becomes less active and consumes less energy. Finally, simply too little exercise alone can lead to a dog becoming overweight.

You can use the following rule of thumb to check whether your dog is overweight: you should be able to feel its ribs, but not see them. If you can't feel its ribs then your dog is much too fat. Overweight dogs live a passive life, they play too little and tire

quickly. They also suffer from all kinds of medical problems (problems in joints and heart conditions). They usually die younger too.

So it's important to make sure your dog doesn't get too fat. Always follow the guidelines on food packaging. Adapt them if your dog is less active or gets lots of snacks. Try to make sure your dog gets plenty of exercise by playing and running with it as much as you can. If your dog starts to show signs of putting on weight you can switch to a low-calorie food. If it's really too fat and reducing its food quantity doesn't help, then a special diet is the only solution.

Caring for your Jack Russell

Good (daily) care is extremely important for your dog. A well cared for dog is less likely to become ill.

Caring for your dog is not only necessary but also a pleasure. Master and dog are giving each other some attention, and it's an excellent opportunity for a game and a cuddle.

The coat

Caring for your dog's coat involves regular brushing and combing, together with checking for parasites such as fleas.
How often a dog needs to be brushed and combed depends on the length of its coat. Once or twice a month is sufficient for a Jack Russell. Use the right equipment for taking care of the coat. Combs should not be too sharp and you should use a rubber or natural hairbrush. Always comb from the head back towards the tail, following the direction of the

hair. If you get a puppy used to being brushed from an early age, it will enjoy having its coat cared for. Only bath a dog when it's really necessary. Always use a special dog shampoo and make sure it doesn't get into the dog's eyes or ears. Rinse the suds out thoroughly. A vet can prescribe special medicinal shampoos for some skin conditions. Always follow the instructions to the letter. Make sure your Jack Russell is dry before letting it outdoors again. Even dogs can catch a cold!

Good flea prevention is highly important to avoid skin and coat problems. Fleas must be treated not only on the dog itself but also in its surroundings (see the chapter on Parasites). Coat problems can also occur due to an allergy to certain food substances. In such cases, a vet can prescribe a hypo-allergenic diet.

Teeth

A dog must be able to eat properly to stay in good condition, so it needs healthy teeth. Check its teeth regularly. Get in touch with your vet if you suspect that all is not well. Regular feeds of hard dry food can help keep your dog's teeth clean and healthy. There are special dog chews on the market that help prevent plaque and help keep the animal's breath fresh, such as Nylabone.

What really helps is to regulary brush your dog's teeth. You can use special toothbrushes for dogs, but a finger wrapped in a small piece of gauze will also do the job. Get your dog used to having its teeth cleaned at an early age and you won't have problems.

You can even teach an older dog to have its teeth cleaned. With a dog chew as a reward it will certainly be happy.

Nails

On a dog that regularly walks on hard surfaces, its nails usually grind themselves down. In this case there's no need to clip their nails. But it wouldn't do any harm to check their length now and again, especially on dogs that don't get out on the streets often. Using a piece of paper, you can easily see whether its nails are too long. If you can push the paper between the nail and the ground when the dog is standing, then the nail is the right length.

Nails that are too long can bother a dog. It can injure itself when scratching, so they must be kept trimmed. You can buy special nail clippers in pet shops. Be careful not to clip back too far as you could damage the skin around the nail, which can bleed profusely. If you feel unsure, have this necessary task done by a vet or a professional groomer.

Special attention is needed for the dewclaw, this being the nail on the inside of the hind leg. Clip this nail back regularly, otherwise it can get caught and become damaged.

Eyes

A dog's eyes should be cleaned regularly. Discharge gets into the corners of the eye. You can easily remove it by wiping it downward with your thumb. If you don't like doing that, use a piece of tissue or toilet paper.

Keeping your dog's eyes clean will take only a few seconds a day, so do it every day. If the discharge becomes yellow this could point to an irritation or infection. Eye drops (from your vet) will quickly solve this problem.

Ears

The ears are often forgotten when caring for dogs, but they must be checked at least once a week. If its ears are very dirty or have too much wax, you must clean them. This should preferably be done with a clean cotton cloth, moistened with lukewarm water or baby oil. Cotton wool is not suitable due to the fluff it can leave behind. **NEVER** enter the ear canal with an object.

If hairs inside the ears cause problems, then it's better to remove them. Carefully pull them out using your thumb and index finger.

If you do neglect cleaning your dog's ears there's a substantial risk of infection. A dog that is constantly scratching at its ears might be suffering from dirty ears, an ear infection or ear mites, making a visit to the vet essential.

Bringing up your Jack Russell

It is very important that your dog is properly brought up and is obedient Not only will this bring you more pleasure, but it's also nicer for your environment.

A Jack Russell terrier is a dominant dog with a strong character. It is definitely not easy to handle and needs a firm hand. This comes from its origins as a 'low' hunting dog. Such a dog must be tough and brave, independent, self-sufficient, intelligent, and able to bite hard and quickly. The Jack Russell certainly possesses these characteristics to the full. It needs a thorough upbringing, bringing out the traits it needs as a family pet, while keeping the undesirable side effects of its hunting instincts under control.

A puppy can learn what it may and may not do by playing. Rewards and consistency are important tools in bringing up a dog. Reward it with your voice, a stroke or something tasty and it will quickly learn to obey. A puppy training course can also help you along the way.

(Dis)obedience

If a lively, self-willed dog like a Jack Russell is not brought up properly, it will often seize its opportunity and be disobedient. A dog that won't obey you is not just a problem for you, but also for your surroundings. It's therefore important to avoid unwanted behaviour. In fact, this is what training your dog is all about, so get started early. 'Start 'em young!' applies to dogs too. An untrained dog is not just a nuisance but can also cause dangerous situations by running into the road, chasing joggers or jumping at people. A dog must be trained out of this undesirable behaviour as uickly as possible. The longer ou let it go on, the more difficult will become to correct. The best ing to do is to attend a special bedience course. This won't only elp to correct the dog's behaviur, but its owner also learns how) handle undesirable behaviour at ome. A dog must not only obey s master during training, but at ome too.

lways be consistent when traiing good behaviour and correcng annoying behaviour. This neans a dog may always behave 1 a certain way, or must never ehave that way. Reward it for ,ood behaviour and never punish after the fact for any wrongoing. If your dog finally comes fter you've been calling it a long ime, then reward it. If you're ngry because you had to wait so ong, it may feel it's actually being unished for coming. It will probably not obey at all the next time or fear of punishment. ry to take no notice of undesirale behaviour. Your dog will pereive your reaction (even a negative one) as a reward for this behaiour. If you need to correct the log, then do this immediately.

ewards for good behaviour are, y far, preferable to punishment; hey always get a better result.

House-training

he very first training (and one of he most important) that a dog

needs is house-training. The basis for good house-training is keeping a good eye on your puppy. If you pay attention, you will notice that it will sniff a long time and turn around a certain spot before doing its business there. Pick it up gently and place it outside, always at the same place. Reward it abundantly if it does its business there.

Another good moment for housetraining is after eating or sleeping. A puppy often needs to do its business at these times. Let it relieve itself before playing with it, otherwise it will forget to do so and you'll not reach your goal. For the first few days, take your puppy out for a walk just after it's eaten or woken up. It will quickly learn the meaning, especially if it's rewarded with a dog biscuit for a successful attempt. Of course, it's not always possible to go out after every snack or snooze. Lay newspapers at different spots in the house. Whenever the pup needs to do its business, place it on a newspaper. After some time it will start to look for a place itself. Then start to reduce the number of newspapers until there is just one left, at the front or back door. The puppy will learn to go to the door if it needs to relieve itself. Then you put it on the lead and go out with it. Finally you can remove the last newspaper. Your puppy is now house-trained. One thing that certainly won't work is punishing an accident after the fact. A dog

whose nose is rubbed in its urine or its droppings won't understand that at all. It will only get frightened of you. Rewarding works much better than punishment. An indoor kennel or cage can be a good tool in helping with house-training. A puppy won't foul its own nest, so a kennel can be a good solution for the night, or during periods in the day when you can't watch it. But a kennel must not become a prison where your dog is locked up day and night.

Basic obedience

The basic commands for an obedient dog are those for sit, lie down, come and stay. But a puppy should first learn its name. Use its name as much as possible from the first day on followed by a friendly 'Come!'. Reward it with your voice and a stroke when it comes to you. Your puppy will quickly recognise the intention and has now learned its first command in a playful manner. Don't appear too strict towards a young puppy, and don't always punish it immediately if it doesn't always react in the right way. When you call your puppy to you in this way have it come right to you. You can teach a pup to sit by holding a piece of dog biscuit above its nose and then slowly moving it backwards. The puppy's head will also move backwards until its hind legs slowly go down. At that moment you say 'Sit!'. After a few attempts, it will quickly know this nice game. Use the 'Sit!' command before giving your dog its food,

putting it on the lead, or before it allowed to cross the road.

Teaching the command to lie down is similar. Instead of movin the piece of dog biscuit backwards, move it down vertically until your hand reaches the ground and then forwards. The dog will also move its forepaws forwards and lie down on its own At that moment say 'Lie down!' This command is useful when yo want a dog to be quiet.

Two people are needed for the 'Come!' command. One holds th dog back while the other runs away. After about fifteen metres, he stops and enthusiastically call 'Come!'. The other person now lets the dog go, and it should obe the command at once. Again you reward it abundantly. The 'Come command is useful in many situa tions and good for safety too.

A dog learns to stay from the sitting or lying position. While it's sitting or lying down, you give the command 'Stay!' and then step back one step. If the dog moves with you, quietly put it back in position, without getting angry. If you do react angrily, you're actually punishing it for coming to you, and you'll only confuse your dog. It can't understand that coming is rewarded one time, and punished another. Once the dog stays nicely reward it abundantly. Practise this exercise with increasing distances (at first no more than one metre). The 'Stay!' command is useful when getting out of the car.

Courses

Obedience courses to help you bring up your dog are available across the country. These courses are not just informative, but also fun for dog and master.

With a puppy, you can begin with a puppy course. This is designed to provide the basic training. A puppy that has attended such a course has learned about all kinds of things that will confront it in later life: other dogs, humans, traffic. The puppy will also learn obedience and to follow a number of basic commands. Apart from all that, attention will be given to important subjects such as brushing, being alone, travelling in a car, and doing its business in the right places.

The next step after a puppy course is a course for young dogs. This course repeats the basic exercises and ensures that the growing dog doesn't learn bad habits. After this, the dog can move on to an obedience course for full-grown dogs. For more information on where to find courses in your area, contact your local dog club. You can get its address from the Kennel Club of Great Britain in London. In some areas, the RSPCA organises obedience classes and your local branch may be able to give you information.

Play and toys

Jack Russell terriers are lively, active dogs that love to play and work. They never have to be asked twice. If you encourage a Jack Russell too much, it will become over-enthusiastic and you'll never be able to stop it again.

There are various ways to play with your dog, You can romp and run with it, but also play a number of games, such as retrieving, tug-of-war, hide-and-seek and catch. A tennis ball is ideal for retrieving, you can play tug-of-war with an old sock or a special tugging rope. Start with tug-of-war only when your dog is a year old. A puppy must first get its second teeth and then they need several months to strengthen. There's a real chance of your dog's teeth becoming deformed if you start too young. You can use almost

anything for a game of hide-and-seek. A frisbee is ideal for catching games. Never use too small a ball for games. It can easily get lodged into the dog's throat.

Play is extremely important. Not only does it strengthen the bond between dog and master, but it's also healthy for both. Make sure that you're the one that ends the game. Only stop when the dog has brought back the ball or frisbee, and make sure you always win the tug-of-war. This confirms your dominant position in the hierarchy. Use these toys only during play so that the dog doesn't forget their significance. When choosing a special dog toy, remember that dogs are hardly careful with them.

So always buy toys of good quality that a dog can't easily destroy.

Be very careful with sticks and twigs. The latter, particularly, can easily splinter. A splinter of wood in your dog's throat or intestines can cause awful problems. Throwing sticks or twigs can also be dangerous. If they stick into the ground a dog can easily run into them with an open mouth.

If you would like to do more than just play games, you can now also play sports with your dog. For people who want to do more, there are various other sporting alternatives such as Flyball, Agility and Obedience.

Aggressiveness

It can happen that a Jack Russell can sometimes be difficult with other animals or people, so it's good to understand more about the background of aggression in dogs.

There are two different types of aggressive behaviour: The anxious-aggressive dog and the dominant-aggressive dog. An anxious-aggressive dog can be recognised by its pulled back ears and its low position. It will have pulled in its lips, baring its teeth. This dog is aggressive because it's very frightened and feels cornered. It would prefer to run away, but if it can't then it will bite to defend itself. It will grab its victim anywhere it can. The attack is usually brief and, as soon as the dog can see a way to escape, it's gone. In a confrontation with other dogs, it will normally turn out as the loser. It can become even more aggressive once it's realised that people or other dogs are afraid of it. This behaviour cannot be corrected just like that. First you have to try and understand what the dog is afraid of. Professional advice is a good idea here because the wrong approach can easily make the problem worse. Because Jack Russells are such exceptionally fearless dogs, anxious-aggressive behaviour rarely occurs in this breed.

The dominant-aggressive dog's body language is different. Its ears stand up and its tail is raised and stiff. This dog will always go for its victim's arms, legs or throat. It is extremely self-assured and highly placed in the dog hierarchy. Its attack is a display of power rather than a consequence of fear. This dog needs to know who's boss. You must bring it up rigorously and with a strong hand. An obedience course can help. Jack Russells are dominant dogs, and almost all the aggression they do display is a result of this dominance. Jack Russell terriers will often act aggressively towards other dogs, especially when they're on the lead. As small as they are, they know almost no fear, but on the lead, protected by their master, they feel totally invincible. However, it's particularly unpleasant when your dog barks fanatically at any passer-by with a dog, so it's important to correct your dog rigorously as soon as (or better before) it starts to do this. A short lead with a choke-chain is a good tool here. If an adult dog has learnt this habit, it can almost never be corrected again.

Unfortunately, a Jack Russell will sometimes get involved in a fierce fight, often even with a bigger dog.

A dog may also display aggressive behaviour because it's in pain. This is a natural defensive reaction. In this case try to resolve the dog's fear as far as possible.

Reward it for letting you get to the painful spot. Be careful, because a dog in pain may also bite its master! Muzzling it can help prevent problems if you have to do something that may be painful. Never punish a dog for this type of aggression!

Fear

Jack Russell terriers know fear only in exceptional circumstances. The source of anxious behaviour can often be traced to the first weeks of a dog's life. A shortage of new experiences during this important phase (also called the 'socialisation phase') has great influence on its later behaviour. A dog that never encountered humans, other dogs or animals during the socialisation phase will be afraid of them later. This fear is common in dogs brought up in a barn or kennel, with almost no contact with humans. As we saw, fear can lead to aggressive behaviour, so it's important that a puppy gets as many new impressions as possible in the first weeks of its life. Take it with you into town in the car or on the bus, walk it down busy streets and allow it to have plenty of contact with people, other dogs and other animals.

It's a huge task to turn an anxious, poorly socialised dog into a real pet. It will probably take an enormous amount of attention, love, patience and energy to get such an animal used to everything around

it. Reward it often and give it plenty of time to adapt and, over time, it will learn to trust you and become less anxious. Try not to force anything, because that will always have the reverse effect. Here too, an obedience course can help a lot. A dog can be especially afraid of strangers. Have visitors give it something tasty as a treat. Put a can of dog biscuits by the door so that your visitors can spoil your dog when they arrive. Here again, don't try to force anything. If the dog is still frightened, leave it in peace.

Dogs are often frightened in certain situations; well-known examples are thunderstorms and fireworks. In these cases try to ignore their anxious behaviour. If you react to their whimpering and whining, it's the same as rewarding it. If you ignore its fear completely, the dog will quickly learn that nothing is wrong. You can speed up this 'learning process' by rewarding its positive behaviour.

Rewarding

Rewarding forms the basis for bringing up a dog. Rewarding good behaviour works far better than punishing bad behaviour and rewarding is also much more fun. The opinions on how to bring up dogs have gradually changed. In the past the proper way to correct bad behaviour was a sharp pull on the lead. Today, experts view rewards as a positive incentive to

get dogs to do what we expect of them. There are many ways to reward a dog. The usual ways are a stroke or a friendly word, even without a tasty treat to go with it. However, with a Jack Russell, you need to be cautious with rewards in the form of food, because it's fixated on food. Knowing that its master has something tasty in his pocket will totally distract it. If you're unlucky it may jump at you if it thinks you're about to pull something nice out of your pocket. During training, a dog biscuit will work wonders, but generally a Jack Russell never needs encouragement. It's enthusiastic enough without a biscuit. Another form of reward is play. Whenever a dog notices that you have a ball in your pocket, it won't go far from your side. As soon as you've finished playing, put the ball away. This way your dog will always do its best in exchange for a game.

Despite the emphasis you put on rewarding good behaviour, a dog can sometimes be a nuisance or disobedient. You must correct such behaviour immediately. Always be consistent: once 'no', always 'no'.

Barking

Dogs which bark too much and too often are a nuisance for their surroundings. A dog-owner may tolerate barking up to a point, but neighbours are often annoyed by the unnecessary noise. Don't encourage your puppy to bark and yelp. Of course, it should be able to announce its presence, but if it goes on barking it must be called to order with a strict 'Quiet!'. If a puppy fails to obey, just hold its muzzle closed with your hand.

A dog will sometimes bark for long periods when left alone. It feels threatened and tries to get someone's attention by barking. There are special training programmes for this problem, where dogs learn that being alone is nothing to be afraid of, and that their master will always return.

You can practise this with your dog at home. Leave the room and come back in at once. Reward your dog if it stays quiet. Gradually increase the length of your absences and keep rewarding it as long as it remains quiet. Never punish the dog if it does bark or yelp. It will never understand punishment afterwards, and this will only make the problem worse. Never go back into the room as long as your dog is barking, as it will view this as a reward. You might want to make the dog feel more comfortable by switching the radio on for company during your absence. It will eventually learn that you always come back and the barking will reduce. If you don't get the required result, attend an obedience course.

Breeding

Dogs, and thus also Jack Russells, follow their instincts, and reproduction is one of nature's most important processes.

For people who enjoy breeding dogs this is a positive circumstance. Those who simply want a 'cosy companion' however, do not need the regular adventures with females on heat and unrestrainable males. Knowing a little about reproduction of dogs will help you to understand why they behave the way they do, and the measures you need to take when this happens.

Liability

Breeding dogs is much more than simply 1+1= many. If you're planning to breed with your Jack Russell, be on your guard, otherwise the whole affair can turn into a financial drama because, under the law, a breeder is liable for the 'quality' of his puppies.

The breed clubs place strict conditions on animals used for breeding. They must be examined for possible congenital defects (see the chapter "Your Jack Russell's health"). This is the breeder's first obligation, and if you breed a litter and sell the puppies without these checks having been made, you can be held liable by the new owners for any costs arising from any inherited defects. These (veterinary) costs can be enormous! So contact the breed association if you plan to breed a litter of Jack Russells.

The female in season

Bitches become sexually mature at about eight to twelve months. Then they go into season for the first time. They are 'on heat' for two to three weeks. During this period they discharge little drops of blood and they are very attractive to males. The bitch is fertile during the second half of her season, and will accept a male to mate. The best time for mating is then between the ninth and thirteenth day of her season. A female's first season is often shorter and less severe than those that follow. If you do want to breed with your female you must allow this first (and sometimes the second) season to pass. Most bitches go into season twice per year. If you do plan to breed with your Jack Russell in the future, then sterilisation is not an option to prevent unwanted offspring. A temporary solution is a contraceptive injection, although this is controversial because of side effects such as womb infections.

Phantom pregnancy

A phantom pregnancy is a not uncommon occurrence. The female behaves as if she has a litter. She takes all kinds of things to her basket and treats them like puppies. Her teats swell and sometimes milk is actually produced. The female will sometimes behave aggressively towards people or other animals, as if she is defending her young. Phantom pregnancies usually begin two months after a season and can last a number of weeks. If it happens to a bitch once, it will often then occur after every season. If she suffers under it, sterilisation is the best solution, because continual phantom pregnancies increase the risk of womb or teat conditions. In the short term a hormone treatment is

worth trying, perhaps also homeo-pathic medicines. Camphor spirit can give relief when teats are heavily swollen, but rubbing the teats with ice or a cold cloth (moisten and freeze) can also help relieve the pain. Feed the female less than usual, and make sure she gets enough attention and extra exercise.

Preparing to breed

If you do plan to breed a litter of puppies, you must first wait for your female to be physically and mentally full-grown. In any event you must let her first season pass. To mate a bitch, you need a male. You could simply let her out on the street and she will quickly return home pregnant. But if you have a pure-bred Jack Russell, then it certainly makes sense to mate her with the best possible

candidate, even if she has no pedigree. Proceed with caution and think especially about the following: Accompanying a bitch through pregnancy, birth and the first eight to twelve weeks afterwards is a time-consuming affair. Never breed with Jack Russells that have congenital defects, and this also applies to dogs without papers. The same goes for hyperactive, nervous and shy dogs. If your Jack Russell does have a pedigree, then mate her with a dog that also has one. For more information, contact the breed association. You will find the address at the back of this book. The breed associations prohibit breeding with a bitch younger than eighteen months. They advise waiting until the second or third season.

Pregnancy

It's often difficult to tell at first when a bitch is pregnant. Only after about four weeks can you feel the pups in her womb. She will now slowly get fatter and her behaviour will usually change. Her teats will swell during the last few weeks of pregnancy. The average pregnancy lasts 63 days, and costs her a lot of energy. In the beginning she is fed her normal amount of food, but her nutritional needs increase in jumps during the second half of the pregnancy. Give her approximately fifteen percent more food each week from the fifth week on. The mother-to-be needs extra energy and proteins during this phase of her pregnancy. During the last weeks you can give her a concentrated food, rich in energy, such as dry puppy food. Divide this into several small portions per day, because she can no longer deal with large portions of food. Towards the end of the pregnancy, her energy needs can easily be one-and-a-half times more than usual.

After about seven weeks the mother-to-be will begin to demonstrate nesting behaviour and to look for a place to give birth to

her puppies. This might be her own basket or a special whelping box. This must be ready at least a week before the birth to give the mother time to get used to it. The basket or box should preferably be in a quiet place.

The birth

The average litter is between three and nine puppies. The birth usually passes without problems. Of course, you must contact your vet immediately if you suspect a problem!

Suckling

After giving birth, the mother starts to produce milk. The suckling period is very demanding. During the first three to four weeks the pups rely entirely on their mother's milk. During this time she needs extra food and fluids. This can be up to three or four times the normal amount. If she's producing too little milk, you can give both mother and her young special puppy milk. Here too, divide the high quantity of food the mother needs over several smaller portions. Again, choose a concentrated, high-energy, food and give her plenty of fresh drinking water, but not cow's milk, which can cause diarrhoea.

You can give the puppies some supplemental solid food when they are three to four weeks old. There are special puppy foods available that follow on well from the mother's milk and that can easily be eaten with their milk teeth.

Ideally, the puppies are fully weaned at an age of six or seven weeks, i.e. they no longer drink their mother's milk. The mother's milk production gradually stops and her food needs also drop. Within a couple of weeks after weaning, the mother should again be getting the same amount of food as before the pregnancy.

Castration and sterilisation

As soon as you are sure your bitch should never bear a (new) litter, a sterilisation is the best solution. During sterilisation the uterus is removed in an operation. The bitch no longer goes into season and can never become pregnant. The best age for a sterilisation is about eighteen months, when the bitch is more or less fully grown.

A male dog is usually only castrated for medical reasons or to correct undesirable sexual behaviour. During a castration the testicles are removed, which is a simple procedure and usually without complications. There is no special age for castration but, where possible, wait until the dog is fully grown. Vasectomy is sufficient where it's only a case of making the dog infertile. In this case the dog keeps its sexual drive but can no longer reproduce.

Sport and shows

Jack Russells are active dogs that won't be satisfied with the odd leisurely stroll. They will quickly become bored and start to display undesirable behaviour. You definitely need to do things with a Jack Russell.

Sport

If you want to do more with your dog than just play normal games, you can take part in sports with it. Jack Russell terriers seem to have been designed for dog sports. They stand out in a number of disciplines that we will cover here.

Flyball

This is a sport that a Jack Russell can really play to its heart's content. During the competition, teams of four dogs face each other in the arena. The dogs have to race over four obstacles to reach a machine with a slanting plank on its front. By pressing on this plank they launch a (tennis) ball. They pick up the ball and get it back to their master as fast as possible. The team that brings back all four balls first are the winners.

Agility

Agility is also a perfect way for a Jack Russell to work off its enormous energy level. In this discipline, dogs have to cover an obstacle course with, among others, slalom, seesaw, tunnel, hurdles and a fence. The dog, enthusiastically spurred on by its master, has to pass all the obstacles correctly. The dog with the fastest time is the winner.

Races

So-called Jack Russell races are very popular. In some places they are even held as 'official' competitions. The dog that finally gets the highest number of points is awarded the title of 'The Fastest Jack Russell Terrier of the Year'. During a race, four dogs chase a 'quarry'. This is a piece of plastic on a nylon line pulled along the course by a winch. The finish is in an imitation foxhole.

Shows

Even if you're not such a sporty person, you can still be active with your Jack Russell. Visiting a dog show is a pleasant experience for both dog and master, and for some dog-lovers it has become a hobby. They visit countless shows every year. Others find it nice to visit an exemption show with their dog just once. It's worth making the effort to visit an exemption show where a judge's experienced eyes will inspect your Jack Russell and assess it for form, markings, condition and behaviour. The judge's report will teach you your dog's weak and strong points, which may help you when choosing a mate for breeding. You can also exchange experiences with other Jack Russell owners.

Ring training

If you've never been to an exemption show, you will need to know what is expected of you and the dog. Many kennel clubs organise so-called ring training courses for dogs going to an exemption show for the first time. This training teaches you exactly what the judge will be looking for, and you can practise this together with your dog.

Club matches

Almost all kennel clubs organise club matches. These meetings are usually small and friendly and are often the first acquaintance dog and master make with a judge. This is an overwhelming experience for your dog - a lot of its contemporaries and a strange man or woman who fiddles around with it and peers into its mouth. After a few times, your dog will know exactly what's expected of it and

will happily go to the next club match.

Championship shows

Various championship shows take place during the course of the year with different prizes. These shows are much more strictly organised than club matches. Your dog must be registered in a certain class in advance and it will then be listed in a catalogue. On the day itself, the dog is kept in a cage (indoor kennel) until its turn comes up. During the judging in the ring, it's important that you show your dog at its best. The judge gives an official verdict. When all the dogs from that class have been judged, the best are selected. The winners of the various classes then compete amongst themselves for the title Best in Show. When this is finished you can pick up your judging report and any prize you may have won.

If you're planning to take your dog to a club match or show, you need to be well prepared.

You must certainly not forget the following:

For yourself:
• Registration card
• Food and drink
• Safety pin for the catalogue number
• Chair(s)

For your dog:
• Food and water bowls and food
• Dog blanket and perhaps a cushion
• Show lead
• A brush
• Vaccination book and other papers

Of course, your dog must look very smart for the show. The judge will not be impressed if its coat is not clean, and its paws are dirty. The dog must also be free of parasites and ailments. Apart from those things, judges also hate badly brought-up, anxious or nervous dogs. Get in touch with your local dog club or the breed association if you want to know more about shows.

Parasites

All dogs are vulnerable to various sorts of parasites. Parasites are tiny creatures that live at the expense of another animal.

Flea

They feed on blood, skin and other body substances. There are two main types. Internal parasites live within their host animal's body (tapeworm and roundworm) and external parasites live on the animals exterior, usually in its coat (fleas and ticks), but also in its ears (ear mite).

Fleas

Fleas feed on a dog's blood. They cause not only itching and skin problems, but can also carry infections such as tapeworm. In large numbers they can cause anaemia and dogs can also become allergic to a flea's saliva, which can cause serious skin conditions. So it's important to treat your dog for fleas as effectively as possible, not just on the dog itself but also in its surroundings.

For treatment on the animal, there are various medicines: drops for the neck and to put in its food, flea collars, long-life sprays and flea powders. There are various sprays in pet shops that can be used to eradicate fleas in the dog's immediate surroundings. Choose a spray that kills both adult fleas and their larvae. If your dog goes in your car, you should spray that too. Fleas can also affect other pets, so you should treat those too. When spraying a room, cover any aquarium or fishbowl. If the spray reaches the water, it can be fatal for your fish!

Your vet and pet shop have a wide range of flea treatments and can advise you on the subject.

Ticks

Ticks are small, spider-like parasites. They feed on the blood of the animal or person they've settled on. A tick looks like a tiny, grey-coloured leather bag with eight feet. When it has sucked itself full, it can easily be five to ten times its own size and is darker in colour.

Dogs usually fall victim to ticks in bushes, woods or long grass. Ticks cause not only irritation by sucking blood but can also carry a number of serious diseases. This applies especially to the Mediterranean countries, which can be infested with blood parasites. In our country these diseases are fortunately less common. But Lyme disease, which can also affect humans, has reached our shores. Your vet can prescribe a special treatment if you're planning to take your dog to southern Europe. It is important to fight ticks as effectively as possible. Check your dog regularly, especially when it's been running free in woods and bushes. It can also wear an anti-tick collar.

Removing a tick is simple using a tick pincette. Grip the tick with the pincette, as close to the dog's skin as possible, and carefully pull it out. You can also grip the tick between your fingers and, using a turning movement, pull it carefully out. You must disinfect the spot where the tick was, using iodine to prevent infection. Never soak the tick in alcohol, ether or oil. In a shock reaction the tick may discharge the infected contents of its stomach into the dog's skin.

Tick

Worms

Dogs can suffer from various types of worm. The most common are tapeworm and roundworm. Tapeworm causes diarrhoea and poor condition. With a tapeworm infection you can sometimes find small pieces of the worm around the dog's anus or on its bed. In this case, the dog must be wormed. You should also check your dog for fleas, which carry the tapeworm infection.

Roundworm is a condition that reoccurs regularly. Puppies are often infected by their mother's milk. Your vet has medicines to prevent this. Roundworm causes problems (particularly in younger dogs), such as diarrhoea, loss of weight and stagnated growth. In serious cases the pup becomes thin, but with a swollen belly. It may vomit and you can then see the worms in its vomit. They are spaghetti-like tendrils.

A puppy must be treated regularly for worms with a worm treatment. Adult dogs should be treated every six months.

Your Jack Russell's health

The space in this book is too limited to go into the medical ups and downs of the Jack Russell Terrier. But we do want to give some brief information about ailments and disorders that affect this breed more often than other dogs.

Generally a Jack Russell terrier that has been bred by a breeder who is a member of a breed association will be lively and healthy. These pedigree animals don't suffer from breed-specific diseases and are also not vulnerable to hip dysplasia (HD), a disorder that normally affects larger dogs.

Patella Luxation

This is a congenital abnormality that unfortunately is becoming more common in unregistered litters. Breeders that are members of the breed association may not breed with Jack Russells that have Patella Luxation. It occurs in various grades. With grade 1, the condition is latent, and the dog will grow out of it. Grade 1 dogs may still be used for breeding.

With this disorder, the kneecap dislocates beside the joint. A luxated kneecap can be caused by a groove that is too shallow, which

is hereditary, but also by a trauma (accident). In this case the luxation may be coupled with torn ligaments. Luxations can occur in various grades. The amount of difficulty and pain the dog suffers differs from one dog to the other. Luxated kneecaps can be operated on. Smooth floors and unusual movements (chasing a bouncing ball, hopping and turning) are bad for the joints of smaller breeds and puppies.

Minor wounds

The Jack Russell's tendency to crawl in and under things, and to get into fights with other dogs means that it may suffer a (minor) wound now and again, so it's a good idea to have a good supply of antiseptic at home.

Beyond that, the Jack Russell is actually a problem-free, strong dog that will need to go to the vet's less than the average dog.

Breeders' Clubs

Becoming a member of a breed club can be very useful for good advice and interesting activities. Contact the Kennel Club in case addresses or telephone numbers have changed.

The Kennel Club
1 Clarges Street
London UK, W1J 8AB
Telephone: 0870 606 6750
www.the-kennel-club.org.uk/

The Jack Russell Terrier Club of Great Britain
Established in 1974. Formed to promote and preserve the working terrier known as the Jack Russell Terrier. Sec. Ms. Janet Bruten
Email: janet.bruten@jrtc.org.uk
www.jackrussellgb.com

Jack Russell Club of East Anglia
The club aims to promote the Jack Russell and to provide shows throughout the year.
Tel. 01359 231995
Email: jackrussellea@aol.com
Www: jackrussell.org.uk.

The Parson Jack Russell Club
Sec. Mrs R M Hussey Wilford.
Tel: 01905 821440
www.dialspace.dial.pipex.com/town/square/gm72/clubindx.htm
Email: parsonjackrussellterrier@dogclub.co.uk

Internet

A great deal of information can be found on the internet. A selection of websites with interesting details and links to other sites and pages is listed here. Sometimes pages move to another site or address. You can find more sites by using the available searchmachines.

www: jackrussellgb.com
Jack Russell Terrier Club of Great Britain. Formed to promote and preserve the working terrier known as the Jack Russell.

www: jackrussell.org.uk
Jack Russell Club of East Anglia The club aims to promote the Jack Russell and to provide shows throughout the year.

www.jrtaa.org/
The website of the Jack Russell Terrier Association of America.

www.terrier.com
Jack Russell Terrier Club of America. The largest Jack Russell Terrier club and registry in the world. Contains useful information about the breed, including care, training, registry, and shows.

www.the-kennel-club.org.uk
The Kennel Club's primary objective is to promote the general improvement of dogs in every way. This site aims to provide you with information you may need to be a responsible pet owner and to help you keep your dog happy, safe and content.

www.k9-care.co.uk
The Self-Help site for dog owners. A beautiful website with tons of information on dogs. All you need to know about grooming, training, health care, buying a dog, travel and much more.

www.mypetsop.com
A mutilingual website that offers dog care, breeding, and behavior information, vet advice, breeder contacts.

www.thedogscene.com

The Dog Scene: this site is dedicated to pedigree dogs in the United Kingdom. Dog breeds, articles, shopping mall are a number of the issues you can find on this website.

www.pet-insurance-uk.me.uk

Find low cost pet insurance via this UK pet insurance directory.

www.pethealthcare.co.uk

At PEThealthcare.co.uk they believe that a healthy pet is a happy pet. Which is why they've brought together leading experts to create a comprehensive online source of pet care information.

www.dogtraining.co.uk

Your central resource for dog-training, boarding kennels & vets in the UK.

www.waltham.com

WALTHAM is a leading authority in pet care and this site includes extensive information on all aspects of dog care, training, and nutrition.

About Pets

- The Border Collie
- The Boxer
- The Bulldog
- The Cavalier King Charles Spaniel
- The Cocker Spaniel
- The Dalmatian
- The Dobermann
- The English Springer Spaniel
- The German Shepherd
- The Golden Retriever
- The Jack Russell Terrier
- The Labrador Retriever
- The Puppy
- The Rottweiler
- The Siberian Husky
- The Shih Tzu
- The Stafforshire Bull Terrier
- The Yorkshire Terrier
- The African Grey Parrot
- The Canary
- The Budgerigar
- The Cockatiel
- The Finches
- The Lovebird
- The Parrot
- The Kitten
- The Cat
- The Siamese cat
- The Persian cat
- The Chipmunk
- The Dwarf Hamster
- The Dwarf Rabbit
- The Ferret
- The Gerbil
- The Guinea Pig
- The Hamster
- The Mouse
- The Rabbit
- The Rat
- The Goldfish
- The Tropical Fish
- The Snake
- The Tortoise

Key features of the series are:
- Most affordable books
- Packed with hands-on information
- Well written by experts
- Easy to understand language
- Full colour original photography
- 70 to 110 photos
- All one needs to know to care well for one's pet
- Trusted authors, veterinary consultants, breed and species expert authorities
- Appropriate for first time pet owners
- Interesting detailed information for pet professionals
- Title range includes books for advanced pet owners and breeders
- Includes useful addresses, veterinary data, breed standards.

about pets

The Jack Russell Terrier

Name:	Jack Russell terrier
Provisional recognition:	1987 (Jack Russell)
First breed standard:	1990 (Great Britain, Parson Russell terrier)
Country of origin:	England
Original tasks:	Hunting dog
Average life expectancy:	15 years
Shoulder height	male: ideally 36 cm female: ideally 33 cm